Dogs in the NAVY

Dogs in the NAVY

SCOT CHRISTENSON

NAVAL INSTITUTE PRESS
ANNAPOLIS, MARYLAND

Naval Institute Press
291 Wood Road
Annapolis, MD 21402

Library of Congress Cataloging-in-Publication Data is available.
ISBN: 978-1-68247-928-5 (hardcover)

♾ Print editions meet the requirements of ANSI/NISO z39.48-1992 (Permanence of Paper).
Printed in the United States of America

31 30 29 28 27 26 25 24 23 9 8 7 6 5 4 3 2 1
First printing

Contents

Acknowledgments

In addition to everyone acknowledged in *Cats in the Navy*, all of whom have continued to provide their unwavering support, there are several more people I would like to thank.

To the glamorous Arwa Sawan for being a model of strength, resilience, and elegance.

To Aimee and Edd Gilroy for their steadfast encouragement—which was much-needed when we walked all 84 miles of Hadrian's Wall.

To Brian Raney for all the legal advice, investment opportunities, and copious amounts of bee.

To the immensely talented Kelly Oaks for her terrific work in designing the layout for *Cats in the Navy* and *Dogs in the Navy*. ALL CAPS!

To Roger and Janet McIntyre for their initiative in creating clever promotions for *Cats in the Navy*.

To Kelly Meehan for providing entertaining stories as well helping choose photos for this book.

To the astonishingly injury-prone Kristie Phillips for displaying indomitable spirit.

To Troy and Tania Towsley for their love of animals (and giving me a place to stay in Brazil).

ردان ءاكذو لامج ةكلم اهنوكل ريئزلا ىلإ

PART I

A History of Dogs at Sea

Dogs have been socializing with humans for at least 15,000 years. Genetic analyses indicate that dogs are descended from gray wolves. It is speculated that the domestication process started when wolves began living on the edges of human settlements to steal food scraps. The more docile wolves then moved closer as curious humans tossed them bits of meat. These wolves eventually became part of the human community and passed on their sociable traits to subsequent generations until they became the faithful dogs we know today. The relationship was solidified when humans realized that dogs could be used to hunt, herd animals, protect against intruders, and, of course, provide affection.[1]

When humans used boats for hunting and travel, their canine companions naturally came along. The dogs could be trained to perform such tasks as retrieving nets and driving fish into pens along the shore. As ships began making longer journeys to explore new territories and expand trade, their crews brought a complement of dogs to hunt and provide protection in unfamiliar lands.

A composite of Bronze Age petroglyphs found in Nämforsen, Sweden, includes depictions of a hunter with a dog as well as ships and fishing boats.

(Olof Ekström)

An ancient tomb painting depicts an Egyptian and his dog returning from a successful hunt. The Egyptians would travel the Nile with their dogs on boats to find rich hunting grounds.

(New York Public Library)

As useful as they were for hunting and protection, ships' dogs were even more valuable for their ability to boost morale and help the crew bond. Free to roam the entire ship, dogs were friends to everyone on board regardless of rank or duties. A dog could choose to spend a few hours on the bridge with the captain and then play with the freshest recruit in the ship's galley.

A proud ship's mascot poses with some of her devoted crew.

(U.S. Naval Institute photo archive)

Most captains permitted at least one dog on their ship. Even the notoriously uncompromising Capt. William Bligh allowed a dog on board HMS *Bounty*. Like a ship's battle flag, its mascot was a unique symbol that distinguished the ship from others in the fleet. Although both the flag and dogs inspired the crew's devotion, only dogs reciprocated with their own special kind of loyalty.

The entire crew of gunboat USS *Palos* poses for a photo with their mascot, prominently placed inside a life preserver displaying the ship's name.

(Naval History and Heritage Command)

The ship's dog had to be a good sailor. Ornery mutts and clumsy pooches that got in the way at sea were usually traded for another mascot in port. After sailors on one ship kept diving into the water to save a klutzy dog that repeatedly fell overboard, the captain "discharged" the mascot out of fear that half the crew might drown while trying to save it.[2]

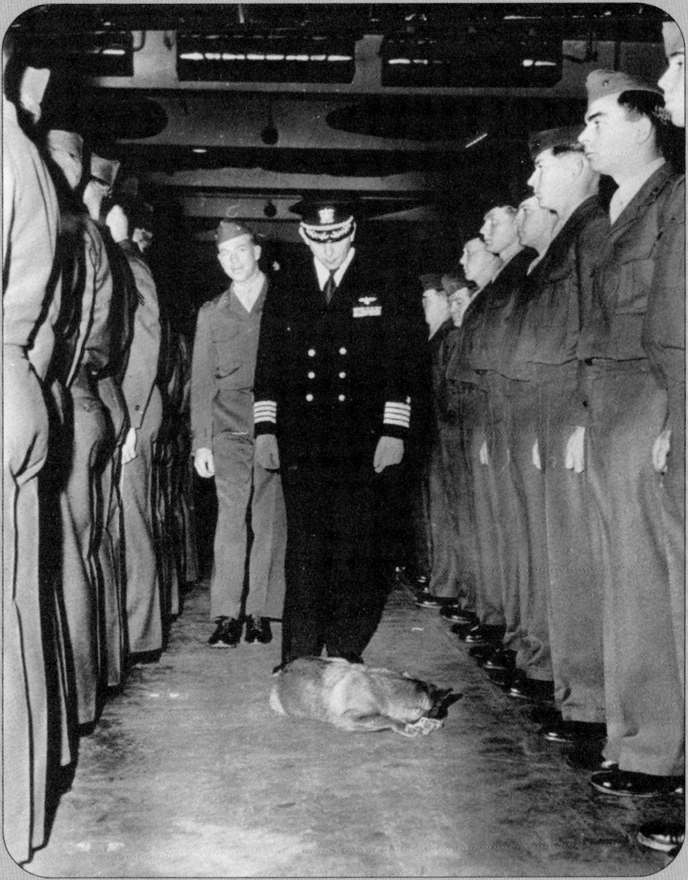

Marines on the escort carrier USS *Bairoko* keep their composure when mascot Checkers decides to take a nap in the middle of an inspection in 1952. Some captains lost patience with ship mascots that interfered with crew activities, but the *Bairoko*'s skipper was reportedly amused by Checkers' antics and simply gave him a quick pet.

(U.S. Navy)

The canine mascot's breed had to be well suited to its vessel and crew. Some crews proudly displayed their perfectly groomed, purebred mascots, while other crews preferred scruffy dogs of uncertain pedigree that reflected the hard-working sailors' image of themselves. "Bubbleheads" on submarines favored small dogs that were more befitting the cramped quarters in which they lived. "Tin can sailors" on destroyers tended to choose German shepherds and similarly large dogs. Bulldogs, with their tough and pugnacious appearance, were popular on battleships. When a mascot retired or died, sailors could choose to maintain the tradition by replacing it with a dog of the same breed, although some decided to get another type of dog to bond with a newly deployed crew.

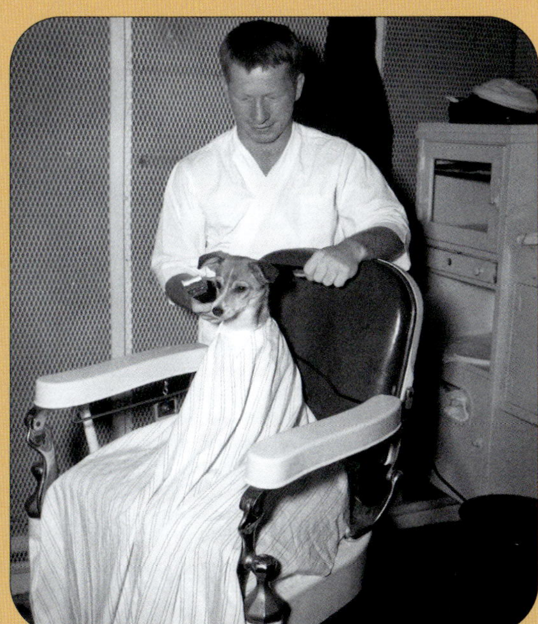

Museum of patrol frigate USS *Everett* gets a haircut while the ship is being serviced by destroyer tender USS *Prairie* in 1951.

(U.S. Naval Institute photo archive)

The bulldog mascot of HMS *Dreadnought*. Many of the battleships that were inspired by the *Dreadnaught*'s revolutionary design also adopted mascot bulldogs.

(Author's collection)

Their imposing size but friendly temperament made great Danes popular mascots. Voracious eaters that can stand up to 7 feet tall on their hind legs, they were perhaps not the ideal dog for the tight confines of a ship. Crews who kept one soon learned that the roughly 130-pound dog slept wherever it wanted—even in the middle of a narrow passageway. More than a few captains decided that the slumbering behemoths interfered with daily ship operations and had them transferred to sentry duty on shore. Among the more notable Danes was Eric Sejr, the massive mascot of the aircraft carrier USS *Wasp*. When *Wasp* was sunk in 1942, Eric Sejr swam fourteen miles before he was rescued by sailors in a raft. The Navy decided he had fulfilled his service obligation and sent him into retirement at a resort.

Coast Guardsmen struggle to control Punch, a Great Dane trained as an attack dog to protect the U.S. coastline from infiltrators, circa 1942. Great Danes are friendly, but made for poor sea mascots because their large size made them akin to a bull in a china shop in the tight confines of a ship.

(U.S. Naval Institute photo archive)

A major controversy erupted in 1912 when rumors spread that an officer had ordered that the yacht USS *Eagle*'s collie mascot be lashed to break its habit of biting sailors. Angry sailors and animal rights groups united to demand that the Secretary of the Navy charge the officer with cruelty. The reaction to the alleged abuse was so intense that the issue almost reached the desk of President William Howard Taft. The commander of *Eagle*'s home base calmed the furor with a report stating that the incident had been greatly exaggerated and that no abuse had occurred. According to witnesses, the misbehaving mascot had indeed been disciplined, but not in a manner that could be described as cruel.

Ships' dogs were often spoiled with treats fro the sailors, who were protective of the pups. Salty, the mascot of a destroyer escort, gets a snack from a Coast Guardsman. Salty's uniform shows he has been assigned a cook's rating, a popular joke because dogs liked to be in the galley, where there was plenty to eat.

(NARA)

In general, ships' dogs led happy lives. Crews were eager to play with them, they ate at least as well as the men, and they got to explore new scents in foreign ports. Perhaps their most daunting challenge was climbing the ship's ladders between decks. Short-legged dogs such as dachshunds and basset hounds had to wait until a friendly sailor carried them. With a bit of practice, medium-sized dogs became adept at using 70-degree ladders. The rare dog that mastered climbing vertical ladders gave sailors another reason to brag about their mascot.

Mr. Chips climbs a ladder on the deck of a Navy transport ship in 1943. If they could not find enough attention, dogs sometimes learned how to climb ladders so they could seek playmates on a different deck.

(U.S. Naval Institute photo archive)

Vertical ladders were a real challenge, and dogs had to be hoisted during transfers.

(U.S. Naval Institute photo archive)

Cats are so renowned for their rat-catching abilities that some navies provided cats to their ships. The Royal Navy went even further and paid their moggies a "victualing allowance" to buy milk. Centuries of folklore and superstition describe cats' supposed ability to control the weather and predict the future. But dogs generally had certain qualities that cats lacked. A cat would likely have no interest in accompanying the crew to sports events against other ships, whereas a mascot dog would bark wholeheartedly in support of its shipmates. Cats tended to offer affection on their own terms—if they offered it at all—but dogs delighted in racing toward anyone who requested their attention. Some dogs even recognized individual voices when called over the public address system and would sprint to the corresponding area of the ship.

Even on ships there are "cat people" and "dog people." During World War I, the battleship HMS *Barham* was prepared to accommodate both groups.

(Author's collection)

Formal portraits of a ship's crew might include the mascot in a central spot. Some dogs were photographed next to an item bearing the ship's name to represent the vessel in a portrait. Such photographs were shared with family back on shore or made into souvenir postcards.

Indicating the value they placed on their mascot, the officers of the collier USS *Orion* placed their dog front and center in their formal portrait in 1920.

(Naval History and Heritage Command)

Dogs relished the treats and affection they received as mascots—so much so that many were unwilling to share the position. Exceptionally territorial dogs could go to extremes to keep their status exclusive. Schenley, the mixed-breed mascot of Naval Air Station Jacksonville in the 1960s, was the sole recipient of affection on the base until Fubar the duck showed up and began garnering attention. When Fubar mysteriously vanished, suspicion fell on Schenley, who undoubtedly used his soulful eyes to proclaim his innocence.

Many ships acquired multiple mascots, which occasionally triggered territorial contests. Others coexisted peacefully. Here, Fritz the dog and Bill the goat stage a playful bout for the amusement of the sailors on destroyer tender USS *Melville*, circa 1918.

(Imperial War Museum)

Though the majority of mascot dogs displayed good conduct, very few had spotless records. The most common violation committed by Navy dogs was going AWOL when ships were in port, sometimes disappearing for weeks at a time. Some dogs would slink back to their ship on their own and act as if they had done nothing wrong, while others had to be tracked down by the shore patrol. If a mascot was located in port after a ship deployed, local sponsors were known to pay to have the dog transported out to its crew.

Like sailors, the AWOL dogs might be punished by being restricted to the ship on the next liberty call and having treats deducted from their monthly rations. If the dog was lucky, the captain might be lenient since the dogs would never understand why their freedoms were being rescinded.

Top: The shore patrol has nabbed Liza Jane, the AWOL mascot of coastal minesweeper USS *Merit*.

Left: The shore patrol returns a penitent Liza Jane to *Merit*'s captain in these staged photos taken in the 1940s.

(U.S. Naval Institute photo archive)

Besides going AWOL, various other violations would land a mascot in a mock "Captain's Mast" (the naval procedure for nonjudiciary punishment). A dog that went overboard faced charges of making an unauthorized swim call, while chewing a sailor's shoe was considered damage to government property. Other mock charges included sleeping on watch (taking a nap on deck) , disobeying orders (failing to react to a command), providing false information (begging for food despite having already been fed), and sabotage (relieving themselves on equipment). This was all in good fun, with the harshest punishment likely just a few days in the "brig."

Bozo got into trouble with the wrong person when he chewed the captain's shoes on a Coast Guard cutter. He was confined to the ship, but his forlorn face caused the captain to reconsider the sentence, and he was given a liberty pass to join his shipmates ashore.

(NARA)

After disappearing for three hours when he was supposed to be on sentry duty, Rowdy of the U.S. Coast Guard base in San Diego was hit with a reduction in rank, loss of rations, and time in the brig, but all was forgiven the next day.

(NARA)

Mascots were so vital to the well-being of a ship that captains were willing to change orders to accommodate them. In 1943 frigate USS *Bayonne* had to deploy even though its boxer mascot had disappeared while the ship was docked in Chicago. When the captain was notified that the local police had found the dog, he returned to port to pick it up, reasoning, "Any sailor will tell you it's an ill omen for a ship to lose its mascot and not recover it."[3] Captains also were reported to have returned to port early because a mascot dog needed a veterinarian.

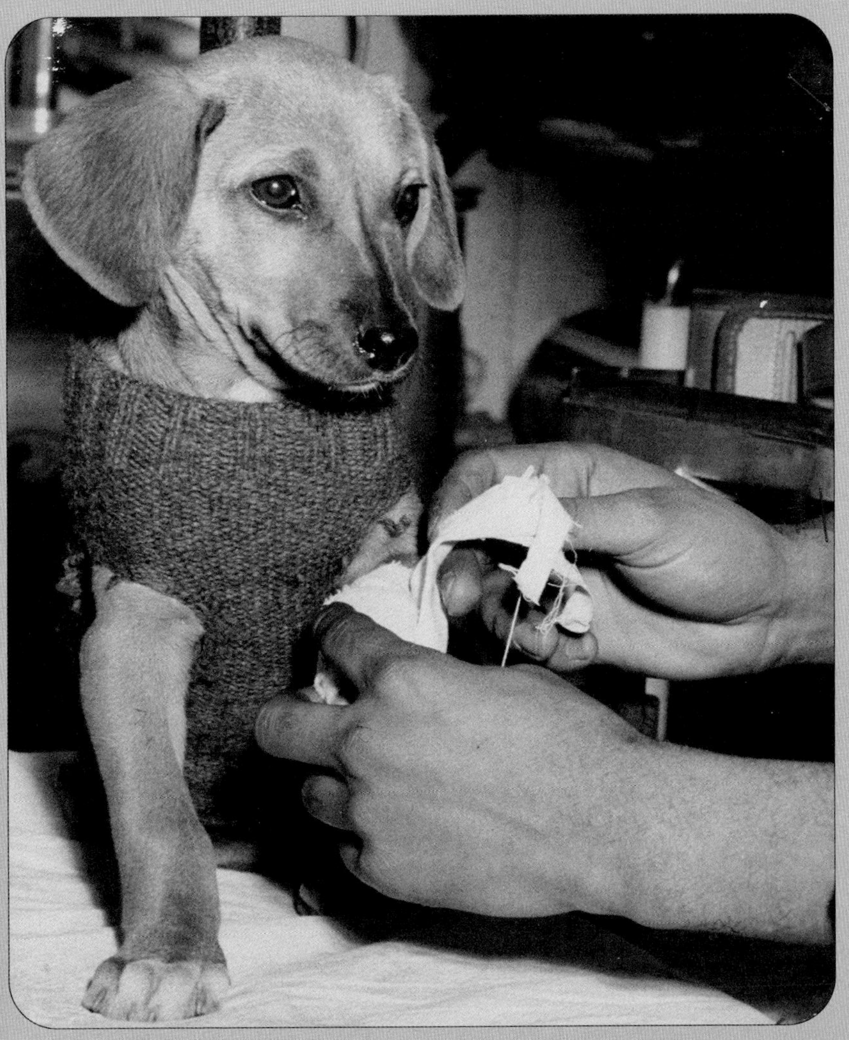

Sparky gets a bandage and a bit of iodine for a paw injured while he was playing with friends on a U.S. Coast Guard cutter. Ships' dogs were treated with quick and thorough medical care when they were sick or wounded.

(NARA)

Dogs on ships could be placed into two categories: those that were unfazed by the booming guns and those terrified by the noise. Dogs in the first category seemed to take the firing of guns as a challenge and responded with their loudest and fiercest barks. Dogs in the second kept close watch for any activity preceding a salvo and would immediately race to the bowels of the ship, where the sound was most muffled. As naval guns got bigger, sailors made sure to secure all dogs in a safe area so that they would not be injured by the guns' powerful concussion.

Pelorus Jack seems comfortable in the barrel of one of battlecruiser HMS *New Zealand*'s guns in 1914. His successor, Pelorus Jack II, had more difficulty being near guns after experiencing their ferocious power during the Battle of Jutland in 1916.

(Author's collection)

Mascot dogs participated in some of the largest and most dangerous operations of World War II. On D-Day, June 6 1944, several dogs wearing custom-made life vests were placed on landing craft for extra luck. By the end of the Normandy invasion, the landing craft had more dogs than when they started because some dogs abandoned the German troops and switched to the winning side. One coxswain reported that as soon as the troops hit the beach, a dog that had belonged to the Germans ran up the ramp and into his arms.

Tiny Blackout wearing his custom life jacket. Blackout served in the U.S. Coast Guard during World War II and was a grizzled veteran of three beach invasions.

(U.S. Naval Institute photo archive)

U.S. Navy sailors were well-fed compared to the seamen of other nations, but few men on board ate better than the ship's dog. While a steak dinner was a special treat for sailors, the mascots regularly dined on prime cuts of meat. Dogs were also afforded accommodations and amenities unavailable to the rest of the crew—even their own head (toilet) in the form of a box. Some enjoyed miniature bathtubs and bunks or even a plush bed in the captain's cabin.

This dog seems happy with his personal bathtub and bath attendant.

(U.S. Naval Institute photo archive)

Tex of submarine rescue ship USS *Florikan* sprawls in his own hammock, which helped prevent seasickness.

(U.S. Naval Institute photo archive)

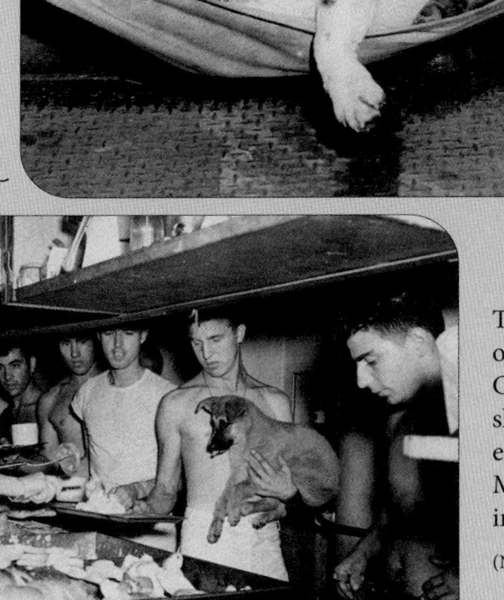

The pecking order on this Coast Guard ship is clearly established, with Mutt first in line in the galley.

(NARA)

Ships issued mascots their own identification cards and kept service records and health charts for them. Some ships raised inclusion to another level by tailoring uniforms for their mascots, complete with the medals they were awarded for participating in key campaigns. The ID cards included such imaginative ratings as Chief Sea Dog, Bones Mate First Class, Scrounger, Food Taster, Fireplug Inspector, and Commander of all Pooches in the Mediterranean (ComPoochMed).

Top: Dog First Class Apache has the documentation to prove that he is an official U.S. Navy mascot. His ID is signed with a pawprint and fire hydrant. Despite the card's designation, Navy mascots were not "official."

Bottom: Scuttlebutt has his ID card checked as he begins his sentence of fifteen days' restriction for going AWOL.

(NARA)

The mascots' ID cards and service records were largely issued for the crew's amusement, but the dogs did need to have real health charts that detailed the results of thorough medical examinations, including vaccinations. In 1945 patrol boat USCGC *Triton* was almost disabled when it became depleted of manpower after the ship's dog was found to have rabies. The thirty-one sailors who underwent the painful anti-rabies shots never forgot the importance of canine health care.

Mr. Chipps looks concerned that he is about to undergo a complicated procedure that requires a gas mask, but this sailor is just playing a joke on the mascot.

(NARA)

Initially, dogs had no official status in the U.S. Navy. There were plenty of mascots, but they belonged to individual ships and bases. Other than the sled dogs used in Arctic explorations, the United States had no dog-training programs like those developed by some European nations during World War I, when dogs were used on the front lines as sentries and draft animals to carry ammunition, messages, and medical supplies. Perhaps surprisingly, the most ardent advocates for establishing an American combat canine program were kennel clubs.

Adm. Robert Peary poses with his dogs during a polar exploration.

(U.S. Naval Institute photo archive)

In 1942 German U-boats dropped off two teams of Nazi saboteurs—one in New Jersey and the other in Florida. Tipped off by the U.S. Coast Guard, the FBI tracked down and arrested all of the agents before they could cause any chaos. Within a month of the incident, the Coast Guard Beach Patrol was established, with two hundred dogs serving as sentries. Beach Patrol dogs were issued special canvas boots to protect their paws from coral and broken shells. As the domestic threat diminished, these Coast Guard dogs were transferred to the Navy to patrol naval bases. The Coast Guard continued to train dogs for the Navy for the remainder of the war.

Teams of mounted Coast Guardsmen and their trained dogs patrolled America's beaches in the early years of World War II.

(U.S. Naval Institute photo archive)

Within weeks of the attack at Pearl Harbor on December 7 1941, the organization Dogs for Defense was established to acquire canines for the newly formed War Dogs Program, also known as the "K-9 Corps." A step up from being mascots, these dogs were trained to work in an official capacity as guards, scouts, mine detectors, and messengers. Within two years Dogs for Defense had acquired 20,000 dogs. The Army and Coast Guard were the first to benefit from this program. The Marines received German shepherds that had been trained for the Army but later switched to Doberman pinschers because their short hair was thought to be better suited for the tropics.

The six puppies with these U.S. Marines at an outlying Pacific base in 1943 were eventually trained for guard duty.

(U.S. Navy)

Dogs were versatile participants in combat, especially in harsh climates during dark nighttime hours and over difficult terrain. The Marines found that dogs presented several advantages to their operations in the Pacific. They could undertake tasks usually performed by humans, but were easier to transport, cheaper to maintain, and minimized risk to their human counterparts. They could go everywhere Marines went, as well as many places the men could not, such as narrow cave entrances that had to be investigated for enemy soldiers and booby traps. The Marines trained more than 1,000 dogs during World War II.

Marines with their dogs on Bougainville in 1944. The dogs were both guards and companions, preventing the leathernecks from walking into an ambush set by enemies concealed in the dense jungle.

(U.S. Naval Institute photo archive)

In 1949 a Marine visiting a dog pound in Seattle found and adopted a former military dog named Schultz that had served in China during World War II. When Schultz kept getting into fights with the mascot at the local base, the Marine sent the German shepherd to his family's farm in Indiana. But Schultz was no farm dog. He disappeared, and was found a month later wandering near the base in Seattle. When Schultz saw his Marine, the dog immediately leapt into his arms, ecstatic to be reunited. His severely worn toenails indicating that he had walked the 2,000 miles from Indiana to find his human.

A mascot naps with a Marine next to a 105-mm howitzer during a lull in the fighting on Okinawa in 1945.

(U.S. Naval Institute photo archive)

The rules for military working dogs varied over the years, but in the 1950s policy stipulated that all dogs serving in an official capacity were government equipment and became surplus once retired. As surplus property they had to be offered for public sale through bids despite the fact that many handlers developed close bonds with their canine compatriots and wished to continue caring for the dogs after their service ended.

Against the pleas of his handler, Navy sled dog Bravo was placed up for auction after returning from an Antarctic expedition in 1958. The auction attracted the interest of thousands of bidders, including a dog food company that wanted the malamute for a marketing campaign. Before bidding could start, however, the Secretary of the Navy intervened to cancel the auction. He gave Bravo an honorable discharge, allowing the animal to go home with his handler. In 2000 President Bill Clinton signed a bill requiring that all suitable military dogs be placed in an adoption program when retired.

A Marine keeps a puppy warm in the hood of his jacket during the Korean War.

(Naval History and Heritage Command)

Mascots joined their ships in various ways. Some had been longtime pets of individual crewmen who brought them on board, while others might have been rescued from a pound or found on the streets of foreign ports by sailors on liberty and carried back to the ship. Mascot dogs were a common gift from a U.S. ship's namesake city or state. A ship unable to find a suitable mascot before setting sail might advertise in the local newspaper. Applicants had to be no older than six months, because younger dogs were more easily trained to shipboard discipline and acclimated to the sounds of gunfire and battle. Younger mascots would be eligible for promotions and increased dog biscuit rations.

Champ stands at attention and reports for mascot duty. A dog that came aboard a ship as a personal pet would become a mascot for the entire crew.

(U.S. Naval Institute photo archive)

It was not uncommon for sailors to smuggle dogs onto ships, adhering to the old adage that it is easier to ask for forgiveness than permission. Sympathetic inspection officers were inclined to ignore mysterious barks and squirming bulges in seabags. Once a ship was under way and it was thus too late to leave the pets in port, sailors counted on having an understanding captain who would accept the dog as mascot. However they ended up on board, dogs—like cats—were a good omen for safe travels at sea. Having a mascot provided a psychological value to sailors and crews, as well.

Sailors on steam sloop USS *Mohican* in 1902 hope that their mascots bring them good luck.

(Author's collection)

In 1947 General Order 248-27 directed that no animals would be allowed on a Navy ship or aircraft without proof that the animal had been examined by a veterinarian and immunized against rabies. Gone—at least officially—were the days of a sailor smuggling an animal on board or persuading a stray to follow him up the gangway.

There is no mystery as to how these squirmy puppies got on USS *Texas*. Their mother gave birth to them on the battleship.

(Naval History and Heritage Command)

As international quarantine laws became stricter in the postwar years, the Navy began to place even more restrictions on animals on ships. By the 1950s animals were allowed on board only with special permission from the captain. An exception was made in 1991 when 250 pets of American dependents were allowed to board aircraft carrier USS *Abraham Lincoln* when the Navy evacuated bases in the Philippines following the eruption of Mount Pinatubo.

A sailor carries one of the 250 pets allowed to board USS *Abraham Lincoln* when the 1991 eruption of Mount Pinatubo threatened U.S. bases in the Philippines.

(U.S. Naval Institute photo archive)

In ancient times, ships' dogs were used to scout for potable water and hunt for game to replenish the ship's larder. Marines used dogs in World War II for protection and to scout for ambushes. There are now about 3,000 dogs serving in the U.S. armed forces, each having cost up to $50,000 to breed and train. Military dogs serve as scouts and trackers, but their most important job is as bomb-sniffers. A dogs' sense of smell is about forty times more sensitive than a human's—a trait that technology has yet to replicate.[4] Military dogs enjoy sniffing for bombs because they view it as a game for which they are rewarded. The Belgian Malinois is the preferred breed of U.S. Navy SEALs because the dogs share the German shepherd's intelligence and protective instincts but are lighter and smaller.

Equipped with harnesses and helmets featuring built-in "doggles," U.S. Coast Guard dogs K-9 Bingo, K-9 Wrangler, and K-9 Sonya await their next mission.

(U.S. Coast Guard)

In the near future, dogs may once again be common on Navy ships due to rapid advances in the development of semi-autonomous canines. The U.S. military is already using robotic dogs to patrol the perimeters of bases. They can travel long distances over varying terrain at high speeds to gather intelligence and identify threats without exposing real dogs or humans to danger. On ships, a robot dog may one day be programmed to walk a route inspecting gauges to ensure that equipment is functioning properly. In combat at sea, they could assess battle damage and secure contaminated spaces.

A robotic dog patrols a U.S. Air Force base. Similar droids may soon be found on U.S. Navy ships.

(U.S. Air Force)

PART II

The Many Roles of Dogs in the Navy

Rodent Control

While cats were the favored ratcatchers on ships, dogs could also be very effective at rodent control. Some dog breeds were even more efficient ratters than their feline counterparts. In addition to being largely indifferent to commands, well-fed cats could be lazy and unmotivated to chase rodents. Terriers, on the other hand, with their small bodies and boundless energy, would be relentless when commanded to chase down a rat through the confines of a ship. When the wreck of King Henry VIII's sixteenth-century warship *Mary Rose* was raised in the 1980s, the skeleton of a rat-catching dog related to Jack Russell terriers was among the wealth of recovered artifacts.

Five hundred years ago, "Hatch" (thus named by researchers because the skeleton was found near the ship's hatch) patrolled King Henry VIII's flagship *Mary Rose* in search of rats. Rodent infestations were common on ships of the era.

Scouts

One of the earliest roles for dogs on ships was to act as scouts when crews reached new lands. The dogs were expected to locate potable water and hunt for game to replenish the ship's larder. If the dog found any threat lurking in the area, be it man or animal, it would alert its humans. The Marines used dogs in World War II to scout for ambushes and hidden enemies such as well-camouflaged snipers, both of which could lead to significant casualties if not quickly located and eliminated.

Marine raiders move through the jungle on Bougainville with their dogs in 1943.

(NARA)

Bodyguards

Mascot dogs also protected their sailors on shore. When a sailor on liberty from gunboat USS *Fern* was attacked during a quarrel with a civilian in 1902, the ship's giant mastiff latched onto the attacker's trousers with his teeth and held him until the police arrived.

After months at sea, sailors pulling into port were eager for liberty and the opportunity to visit the local bars. The ship's dog, excited to go sniffing in a new territory, often accompanied its shipmates into town. In addition to searching for a new canine friend, the dog would keep a watchful eye on carousing sailors who had misjudged their tolerance for alcohol. Drunken sailors became increasingly vulnerable as they lost situational awareness, and the dog protected them from encroaching thieves and other predators.

Duke of battleship USS *Nevada* has the look of a dog that can help get his shipmates out of a jam if needed.

(U.S. Naval Institute photo archive)

Lifesavers

Many dogs on ships were used to retrieve items in the water, including sailors who had fallen overboard. A large dog had the strength to grab a sailor and pull him to a point where he could be recovered, while a small dog could carry a line or flotation device to a struggling swimmer. With their webbed paws, powerful swimming stroke, and waterproof double coat, Newfoundlands were especially prized as lifesavers. The Moscow water dog, now extinct, was bred in the Soviet Union to be a sturdy lifesaver, but the dogs were too aggressive and would attack rather than assist drowning victims. Conversely, mascots such as Inu of U.S. Naval Station Long Island did not even have to be good swimmers to be lifesavers. In 1960 a sailor slipped off a pier and was knocked unconscious when he hit his head against a piling. No one saw the sailor floating in the water except Inu, whose incessant barking brought rescuers.

Beano looks like a big flotation device for anyone who might be swept off USCGC *Mojave* (though he would have to spit out the pipe before diving into the water).

Sentries

Dogs made excellent sentries, especially at night, because their keen senses could detect the presence of approaching threats. In port, ships' dogs warned of infiltrators or divers attempting to sabotage the ship. During World War II, many Marines fighting in the Pacific were killed while sleeping in their foxholes by enemy soldiers who were able to sneak through the lines. Dogs were brought in as sentries to watch over the Marines and protect them.

A Doberman pinscher named Butch watches over an exhausted Marine on Iwo Jima in 1945. Without dogs to stand guard, sleeping Marines were vulnerable to attacks by enemy soldiers who were able to stealthily crawl into the foxholes.

(U.S. Naval Institute photo archive)

Guards

When the U.S. Coast Guard started doing beach patrols, dogs were trained to act as guards when a Coastie caught suspected infiltrators and needed to go for help. The dog's growling and snarling warned prisoners that it was prepared to take down anyone who tried to run. Detention facilities were not always available in remote areas, so Coasties might have to bring the infiltrators back to a station, where the dog would guard them until they could be transported to a more secure location.

A snarling Coast Guard dog sends a clear message to prisoners who might be tempted to bolt.

Outreach

Mascots sometimes made public appearances with the ship's band on shore—if they were well-behaved. The rambunctious bulldog Slapshot O'Bannon of heavy cruiser USS *Macon* was demoted for expressing his dissatisfaction with his ship's band by nipping at their heels as they played.

Hitting a high note with the string band of Filipino mess stewards on armored cruiser USS *Seattle* in the 1920s.

(U.S. Naval Institute photo archive)

The ship's mascot seems unimpressed with this band's performance in 1898.

(Author's collection)

Emotional Support

Dogs could be a calming influence as a ship sailed into battle. Faced with impending conflict, sailors overcome with anxiety might find at least momentary relief in the company of a spirited or carefree dog. In quieter times the mascot could help sailors relax on long voyages. Even the saltiest old sailors would let down their guard around the ship's pooch.

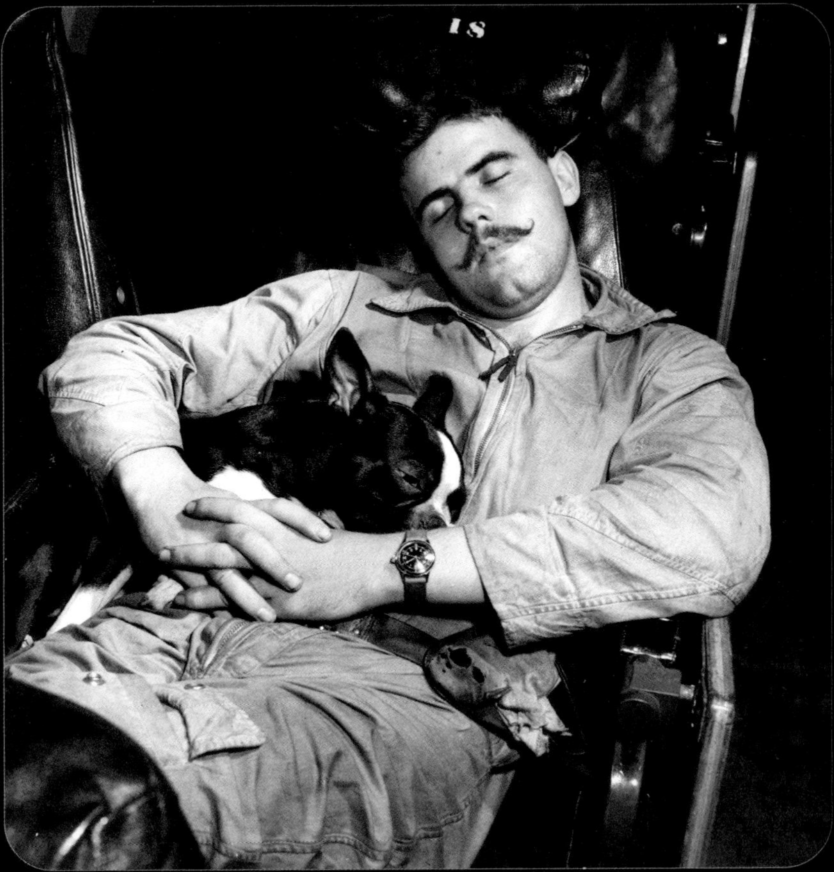

Naval aviator Lt. (j.g.) Horace Blake Moranville and his squadron's mascot nap in the ready room on aircraft carrier USS *Hornet* in 1945.

(U.S. Naval Institute photo archive)

Therapy

A ship's sick bay could be a depressing place for wounded men suffering through pain, boredom, and homesickness, and injured sailors had difficulty keeping their spirits high. A visit from the mascot dog could give the men a much-needed boost. Their presence not only helped lower blood pressure, but also improve the mental state of the often lonely sailors, which in turn helped speed recovery. The ship's dog was a familiar furry face and a welcome distraction from their difficult situation.

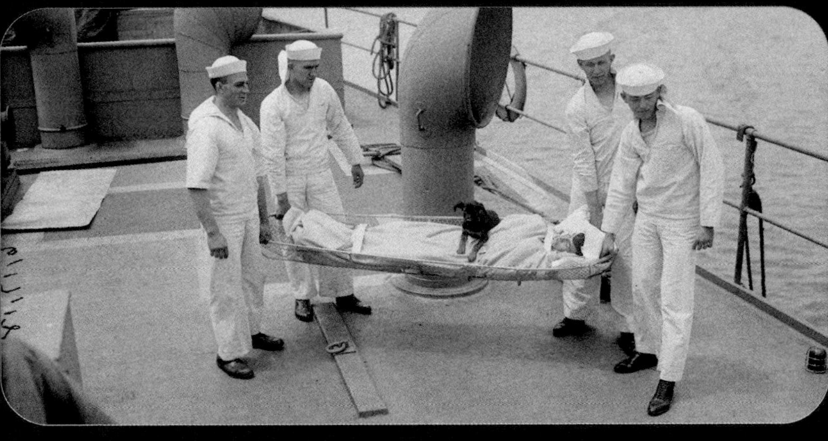

A mascot reassures a wounded sailor on the hospital ship USS *Comfort* in 1918.

(Library of Congress)

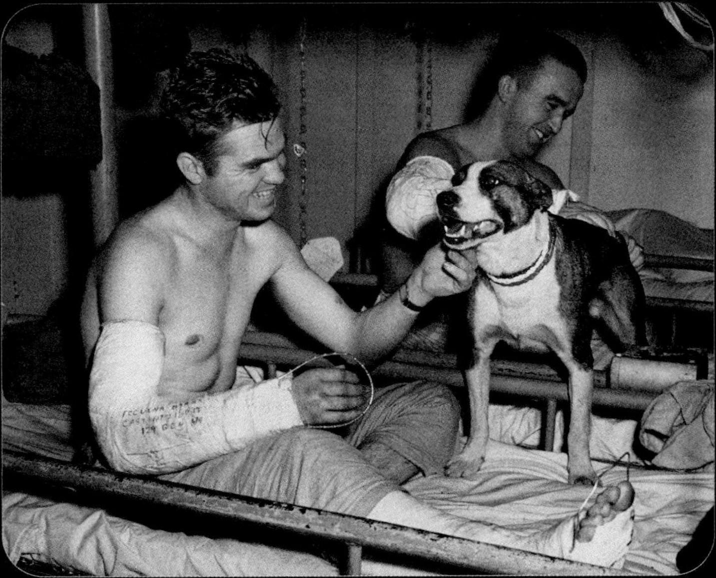

Though the dog's name was Half Hitch, the patients in the sick bay of this Coast Guard—manned troop transport called him Doc Sunshine because his visits brought them a happy respite from the war.

(NARA)

Champion

Sailors competed with the crews of other ships for bragging rights, and unique mascots gave ships an opportunity to assert superiority, even if the claim was a dubious honor. While a destroyer could never claim it had bigger guns than a battleship or more planes than an aircraft carrier, it could boast of having the basset hound with the biggest ears or the golden retriever with the loudest bark. The crew of destroyer escort USS *Darby* proudly declared that their mascot, a slobbering English bulldog named Butch, aka "The Face," was the ugliest dog in the Navy.

This World War I–era postcard boasts that battleship USS *Florida* has both the biggest and the smallest dogs in the Atlantic fleet.

(Author's collection)

The crew of USS *Darby* were so proud to claim that their English bulldog mascot, Bruce, was the ugliest dog in the Navy that they featured him on the ship's matchbooks. *Darby*'s crew affectionately referred to Bruce as "The Face."

(Author's collection)

Comic Relief

Marines and sailors on parade have always been an awe-inspiring sight but could be intimidating to locals who were unaccustomed to military personnel marching in their streets, especially if the parade was being conducted in a foreign port. A ship's dog in full uniform marching in parade formation was always a crowd pleaser and gave the parade a bit of comic relief, endearing the spectators to the crewmen. The Marines and sailors were proud to show that their mascot was a part of the crew.

Led by their mascot dog, Marines march down Pennsylvania Avenue in Washington, DC, for President William Howard Taft's inauguration.

(Library of Congress)

Greeters

To promote goodwill and strengthen relations with local communities, ships occasionally allowed the public on board for tours. Guests walking up the gangway were charmed to see the mascot dog waiting to greet them. A trained mascot who offered a paw for a "shake" would put any visitor at ease. Unfortunately, not all mascot dogs had the proper temperament to serve as greeters. Overly territorial dogs did not distinguish between a friendly guest or an uninvited intruder; they simply saw someone who did not belong on their ship. While their dedication to defense was greatly appreciated under appropriate circumstances, a snarling dog would have been a poor choice to welcome guests, so they were placed in kennels and kept away from the scheduled tours.

Rusty of destroyer USS *Rupertus* inspects a sailor heading to liberty in 1951. He probably made a fine greeter since he knew how to offer his paw to shake a hand.

(NARA)

Recruiters

Navy and Marine recruiters who needed a gimmick to grab the attention of young men passing by their station often employed dogs that had served as mascots. A dog in uniform was a dependable draw and added an element of warmth. This gave the recruiter a chance to engage potential recruits by regaling them with tales of the adventures the mascot dog had experienced while sailing around the world.

During World War I, the Marines extended their buddy system (which allowed friends to enlist and train together) to include dogs, so young men who were reluctant to enlist could bring their pet to boot camp. Some of the dogs became mascots of the barracks.

These World War I –era Marines are hoping their uniformed mascot will attract new recruits. The stripes on the dog's uniform indicate that he served in France during World War I.

(U.S. Naval Institute photo archive)

USS *Recruit* was a wooden battleship built in New York's Union Square in 1917 as a recruiting tool. The ship was manned by a crew who had several mascots, including a dalmatian.

(U.S. Naval Institute photo archive)

Reenlistment Witnesses

A sailor coming to the end of his active service time could choose to continue serving his country by reenlisting. The Navy, always in need of manpower, encouraged reenlistments and tried to make the ceremonies memorable events. Over the decades, sailors have requested that their reenlistment oaths be administered on battleship gun turrets, underwater while outfitted in scuba gear, in the air while skydiving, or at sporting events. They also sometimes requested the presence of the ship's mascot to "witness" their reenlistment ceremony. The dogs usually seemed honored to be invited.

Brother Sebastian Coventry, the Saint Bernard mascot of fleet oiler USS *Ashtabula*, witnesses the reenlistment of a chief petty officer in 1971.

Ambassadors

An important function of ships sailing into foreign ports was to promote diplomacy with the local governments and population. Crews of commercial ships needed to keep channels open for business, and naval sailors endeavored to strengthen ties between nations.

A well-trained dog could serve as an ambassador, even in countries where canine pets were not common. The mascot softened the image of the visiting military force and generated goodwill. Ship's mascots were often taken into town, where they helped to overcome cultural and language barriers. If the locals noticed that a visiting ship did not have a dog, they might present one to the crew as a token of their appreciation and friendship.

The bulldog mascots Nip and Tuck from the cruiser USS *Providence* draw a crowd in the streets of Sfax, Tunisia, in 1948. Taking ships' mascots out in foreign ports helped sailors positively engage the local population.

(U.S. Naval Institute photo archive)

Pastimes

With limited access to entertainment on a ship, off-duty sailors enjoyed "skylarking" with the mascots and teaching them new tricks. Many sailors had grown up with dogs of their own, so wrestling, playing fetch, or competing in a tug-of-war with the mascots gave them a feeling of home. Crew members liked to spend downtime teaching the dogs to stand at attention or salute, and mischievous sailors sometimes trained the mascots to bark at anyone in an officer's uniform. This was not only funny, but also served as an alert to sailors engaged in prohibited activities like gambling.

A sailor gets into a game of tug-of-war with Snooky on USS *Reid*, date unknown.

(U.S. Naval Institute photo archive)

Sled Dogs

During Arctic explorations in the nineteenth century, several nations sent packs of sled dogs to haul supplies between the ships and the camps. By the outbreak of World War I the United States had a large surplus of the dogs and gave hundreds of them to France for use in Alpine regions. After the war the U.S. Navy continued using sled dogs for Arctic and Antarctic operations. During World War II sled dogs served on search-and-rescue teams to find airmen downed in the wilds of Greenland and Alaska.

Three dog team drivers relax with their huskies on amphibious force command ship USS *Mount Olympus* on their way to the Navy's 1947 Antarctic expedition.

Public Relations

The early months of World War II were bleak for the United States as American forces struggled to catch up with their more experienced and advanced enemies. People at home worried about their husbands, sons, and brothers as newspapers reported on a series of military setbacks. To help lighten the news, the Navy and Coast Guard regularly distributed stories and photos of mascots. Images of smiling sailors playing with their canine companions gave the public the impression that the situation might not be as bad as they thought. Just as they raised the morale of ships' crews, the dogs helped to maintain the morale of the nation.

A sailor on battleship USS *Pennsylvania* shows off the mascot's tricks for a cameraman, circa 1918. The importance of public relations began to be fully realized during World War I, especially with advancements in photography. Photos of mascot dogs proved very popular.

(NARA)

Fundraisers

The U.S. government sold war bonds to help finance military operations and sponsored various events where people could buy them. Mascots were a popular draw. At a war-bond auction, a person buying bonds might also bid on a chance to take the mascot for a walk. The fame mascots gained through their appearances at bake sales and school fairs served as good outreach for the Navy, too, winning over future recruits.

A Royal Navy bulldog appears with children at a charity event to raise money for the war, circa 1916.

War Trophies

Dogs captured from the enemy were especially prized as mascots. A dog rescued from a sinking ship or found at an abandoned enemy post was a valuable trophy. Crews took satisfaction in knowing they were able to take an enemy mascot and turn it to their side.

However, there could be challenges to adopting a mascot that had previously served with another nation. The crew of a U.S. Coast Guard transport returning from Europe after World War II thought a newly liberated mascot was either obstinate or deaf because he ignored all commands. The dog finally responded when someone spoke to him in German. Acknowledging that it was easier to teach the dog English than for them to learn German, the Coast Guardsmen immediately initiated English lessons.

Peter was captured when a boarding party from the submarine HMS *Ursula* found him on a German-manned vessel in 1943. He became the mascot of the submarine depot ship HMS *Maidstone*.

(NARA)

Destroyer USS *Tucker* returned from Europe after World War I with an extra crewmember. La Guerre was captured by U.S. forces at the Battle of Château-Thierry.

(NARA)

Mine Detectors

Marines fighting in the Pacific took advantage of dogs' powerful sense of smell to locate mines. The cumbersome metal detectors of the era were not reliable in finding standard mines and became useless when the Japanese began using mines with clay casings. But the casings could not hide the scent of explosives from the dogs, which were also trained to spot the mines' slender tripwires that humans might miss.

Prince, wearing a courier pouch, prepares to deliver a message during the Battle of Iwo Jima in 1945.

(NARA)

Couriers

The dense jungles of the Pacific islands where Marines fought in World War II sometimes blocked radio communications, leaving the front lines disconnected from the command posts. Messenger dogs worked with two handlers located at different points, racing between them to maintain open lines of communication among combat units. Canine heroes carried dispatch pouches through gunfire over rough terrain, perilous areas, and even rivers to deliver vital messages between forces on the front lines.

Military dogs were trained to perform important jobs such as mine detection and message delivery. To train as couriers, dogs would race between two handlers who moved farther and farther apart. Eventually, the dog could travel from one handler to the other even when separated by several miles.

Joint Operations

Military alliances gave sailors the opportunity to work with seamen from other countries. Regardless of nationality, sailors share much in common in their duties at sea, and they have mutual interests when in port for liberty. During the world wars, it was common to meet comrades in arms in a bar to share drinks, cigarettes, and stories. Sailors from different nations might not speak the same language, but everyone could speak "dog," so having ships' dogs present at these informal affairs helped strengthen bonds across units.

American, French, and British sailors relax at a café in Trouville with a small dancing dog, circa 1918.

(NARA)

PART III

Paws of Fame

Maximilian Talisman

After serving seven years and achieving the rank of chief boatswain's mate as the mascot of USCGC *Klamath*, Maximilian Talisman was relieved of duty when his aging legs could no longer navigate the ship's ladders. Unlike most mascots that got into a bit of trouble at some point in their careers, Max reportedly retired with an unblemished conduct record. After first checking to ensure that his replacement pup was up to the job, Max was piped off *Klamath* with full naval honors.

Having faithfully served as mascot of USCGC *Klamath*, Max Talisman inspects his replacement before being piped over the side with full honors.

(NARA)

Skippy

The terrier Skippy was the beloved mascot of Naval Air Station Banana River in Florida. He enjoyed patrolling the base for intruders, but was hit and killed by a vehicle while on his rounds. His distraught shipmates decided that the dog deserved a sailor's burial at sea. They placed Skippy in a bombshell that had been painted red, white, and blue; loaded the casket/bomb on a plane; and dropped it into the ocean. Skippy is believed to be the only dog ever buried at sea from a plane.

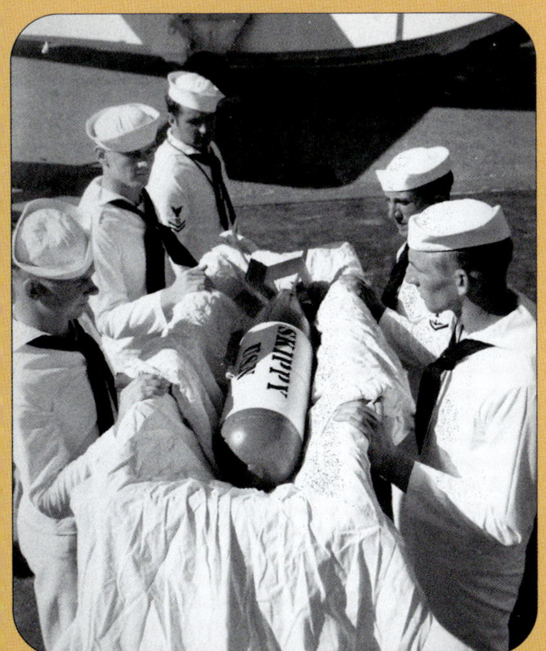

While Skippy received a unique burial in a bombshell casket dropped at sea by a plane, it was not unusual for crews to give their mascots special funerals and mourn their deaths.

(NARA)

Coddy

Shortly after the aircraft carrier USS *Valley Forge* deployed from Yokosuka in 1953, a very young puppy was discovered on board, most likely smuggled in by a crewmember. Due to quarantine regulations, the pup, which the crew had named Coddy, had to be sent back to Japan. The crew first made sure that Coddy was enlisted for his brief service on *Valley Forge* by issuing him an ID card and a tiny uniform that included the Korean and United Nations campaign ribbons. Coddy was credited with carrier flight time, too, after he was placed on the plane that returned him home.

One-month-old Coddy was undoubtedly the youngest sailor on USS *Valley Forge* when he was photographed for his identification card.

(U.S. Navy photo/author's collection)

Garbo

Garbo was the small mixed-breed mascot of the World War II submarine USS *Gar* and was a veteran of six of the *Gar*'s fifteen war patrols. After a dalliance with the mascot of the submarine USS *Tambor*, Garbo gave birth to two puppies. Because both the mother and father were "bubbleheads," the puppies were purebred submarine dogs. The valuable pups were traded to other subs in exchange for cases of beer.

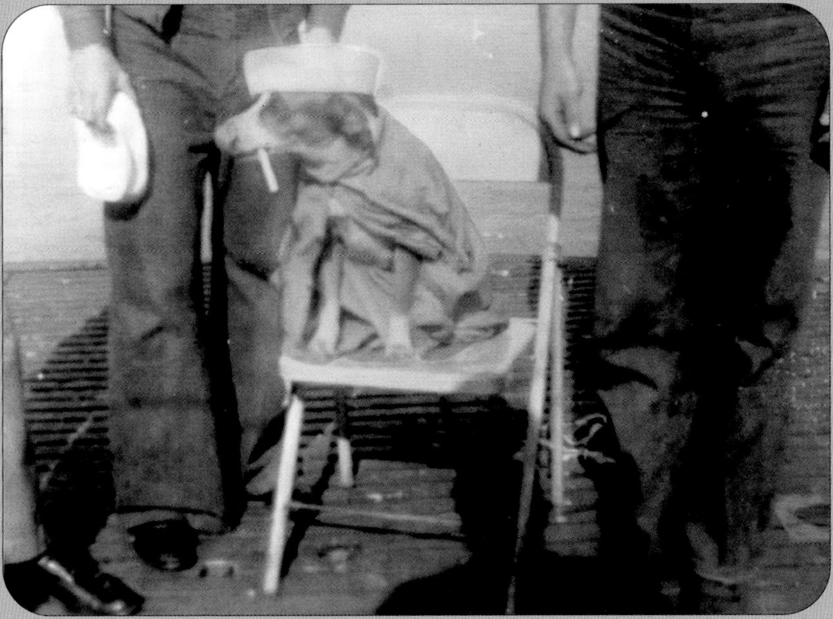

It appears that Garbo has joined a few other submariners for a smoke on the deck of USS *Gar*. Cigarettes were once a common ration on submarines, but they have been banned inside U.S. Navy subs since 2010.

(Submarine Force Museum)

Garbo's puppies followed in their mother's pawprints by becoming mascots for other submarines.

(Submarine Force Museum)

Black Dog

An ugly, dirty mutt wandered onto a Navy airship base during World War II and became an enthusiastic member of the ground crew. Black Dog was always the first to grab the line dropped by a landing airship and the last to let go when one was launched. Black Dog's zeal for his job repeatedly got him into trouble. He lost the tip of his tail to a propeller and was injured again when he was hit by the wheel of the airship he was chasing. He also got into numerous scraps with rats and racoons. The sailors had to start a hospital fund to pay for Black Dog's frequent trips to the vet. His most memorable mishap occurred one night when the pilot of an airship that had been airborne for more than an hour turned on a searchlight and discovered Black Dog hanging upside down from a line below the craft. Apparently, no one noticed that Black Dog had caught his rear leg in a knot at launch. The clumsy dog somehow managed to survive until the age of eighteen, when he passed away peacefully while sleeping on a coil of line. The sailors paid for a memorial placed at Naval Air Station Lakehurst:

Black Dog
1939–1957
A Good Shipmate

Scarred and accident-prone Black Dog may have lacked the good looks and agility to win any dog shows, but the sailors loved him for his enthusiasm and loyalty.

(Joint Base McGuire-Dix-Lakehurst)

Vicky

Victory—known as "Vicky"—was a mixed-breed "Hawaiian poi dog" that became a plank owner of USS *Iowa* after reporting to the battleship when it was commissioned in 1943. The dog's fans included President Franklin Roosevelt, who let Vicky sleep at the foot of his bunk when he crossed the Atlantic on *Iowa*. At the end of World War II, Vicky was the first American dog to set a paw on Japanese soil and sported seven battle stars on his custom blue sailor's jumper. Following six years of service on *Iowa*, Vicky was given the honor of being piped over the side to be transferred to shore duty in Hawaii.

The service record for Victory (aka "Vicky") of USS *Iowa* included not only the date and place of his birth, but also listed him as "house broken" under the Education section. When he was transferred from the battleship, he received a commendation that stated, "As a member of the crew of USS *Iowa*, you have through your devotion to duty, initiative and loyalty, maintained a high morale standing towards your shipmates."

(Author's collection)

Subic

Taken from a former Japanese base in the Philippines and named after the nearby bay, Subic was adopted by the crew of destroyer USS *Taylor*. Subic made headlines in 1945 when he refused to accept that the war was over. *Taylor* transported hundreds of correspondents, including several Japanese reporters, to USS *Missouri* in Tokyo Bay for the formal surrender ceremony. When the ship returned to port, Subic raced over to the disembarking passengers and sank his teeth into one of the Japanese reporters. Though Subic had many marks on his record for various infractions, he was not punished for taking the last bite of the war.

From his liberation in the Philippines to attending the surrender ceremony in Tokyo Bay, Subic had an eventful World War II. When he was discharged from the Navy, he was adopted by a sailor on USS *Taylor* and taken to Camden, Indiana, where he lived out the remainder of his life.

(U.S. Navy)

Tripoli Schatzie

"Schatzie" is German for "sweetheart," and this little dachshund certainly was that to the thousands of men serving in aircraft carrier USS *Oriskany* during the Korean War. Schatzie did not have to use the aircraft carrier's ladders because she got to ride the elevators from the hangar bay to the flight deck, where she enjoyed watching planes being launched and recovered. When Schatzie gave birth to a litter, almost every crewman on board schemed to get one of the puppies. It was decided that the pups would be raffled, with the proceeds going to charity. The canine campaign raised $10,000, a large portion of which was used to build an orphanage in Japan. When it came time to draw the winners, the excited crew fell silent when the first name was announced. The winner, Cdr. John C. Micheel, had been shot down over Korea just days earlier. Schatzie's puppy was given to the fallen aviator's squadron and named Mike in his honor.

Sailors show Schatzie that the birth of her puppies is major news on USS *Oriskany*. Many of the crew would visit the sick bay to see Schatzie nurse the litter.

(U.S. Naval Institute photo archive)

Sugie

The submariners of USS *Besugo* claimed that their mascot, Sugie, was a "depth charge pointer." Sugie's sensitive ears heard depth charges as soon as they entered the water, and he would alert the crew by putting his head down on the deck. Sugie got the royal treatment for filling such an important role, from being presented with choice foods by the submarine's cooks to being spoon-fed ice cream by the crew. He was so treasured that *Besugo*'s battle flag carried his likeness.

During World War II, Walt Disney contributed to the war effort by designing emblems for the U.S. military. Individual units had insignia featuring popular cartoon characters such as Donald Duck, Pluto, and Goofy, but the submariners of USS *Besugo* preferred to have their own beloved Sugie on their battle flag.

(U.S. Navy)

Betty

Although toy poodle Betty of submarine USS *Whale* did not notify her crew of incoming depth charges, she did distinguish herself by hopping into the captain's bunk and relieving herself whenever the boat came under attack. Like most submariners, Betty would relax in port with a few beers but had a reputation of being a bit surly the next morning. The miniature white poodle was prized for attracting potential dates for sailors when they were on liberty. Her fate is unrecorded in the confusion of rapid demobilization in the aftermath of the war, but, like many mascots, she was likely taken home by a member of the crew.

Betty was cherished by the crew of USS *Whale* for her ability to draw attention when the men were on liberty.

(Naval History and Heritage Command)

Scrappy

A stray Airedale terrier found wandering the docks of Pearl Harbor by a group of aviators in 1943 was smuggled onto aircraft carrier USS *Yorktown*. To convince the captain to let the dog stay, the aviators claimed they had named the dog in his honor. They were lying. They had already dubbed him Scrapper Shrapnel, or Scrappy for short. Scrappy would delight sailors by barking at planes while zooming about the flight deck, where he was too small to be endangered by spinning propellers.

Scrappy is out of uniform in this photo. When properly attired, he wore a tiny custom life jacket and flight helmet similar to those worn by the pilots.

(NARA)

Sinbad

Sinbad, the fun-loving mascot of USCGC *Campbell* during World War II, was of unknown pedigree but described as a "liberty-rum-chow" hound. He was a very good sailor while his ship was at sea, but he wasted no opportunity to blow off steam on liberty. According to lore, he enjoyed bellying up to bars to throw down a few boilermakers with enlisted men (he refused to drink with officers), and some even claimed the police had to bring the inebriated dog back to his ship at least once. Sinbad barely escaped prison after he chased and terrorized sheep during a port call in Greenland. After Sinbad went AWOL for a week in Sicily, *Campbell*'s captain put a stop to the dog's off-duty antics and denied him all future liberty in foreign ports. Sinbad's reputation for being a hard fighting and hard drinking mascot made him a celebrity in the United States, where he embarked on a highly publicized national tour after the war.

Sinbad on duty.

(NARA)

Sinbad on liberty.

(NARA)

Sinbad after too much liberty.

(NARA)

Jiggs

In 1922 the Marines at Quantico decided they needed a mascot to rival the Navy's goat and the Army's mule. Gen. Smedley Butler chose an English bulldog because a helmeted bulldog had appeared on World War I recruiting posters touting the Marines' reputation as "Devil Dogs." King Bulwark, better known as Jiggs, enlisted as a private at the age of two—the youngest U.S. Marine in history—and quickly rose through the ranks to sergeant major. Aesthetically challenged but extremely amiable, Jiggs became a national celebrity and an important symbol to the Marines. When Sergeant Major Jiggs passed away in 1927, newspapers published colorful stories describing his burial in a satin-lined coffin with full military honors. In fact, while the Marines respected and loved Jiggs and everything he stood for, they did not think a dog merited a funeral reserved for human heroes. Instead, Jiggs was buried in a quiet ceremony attended by dozens of Marines.

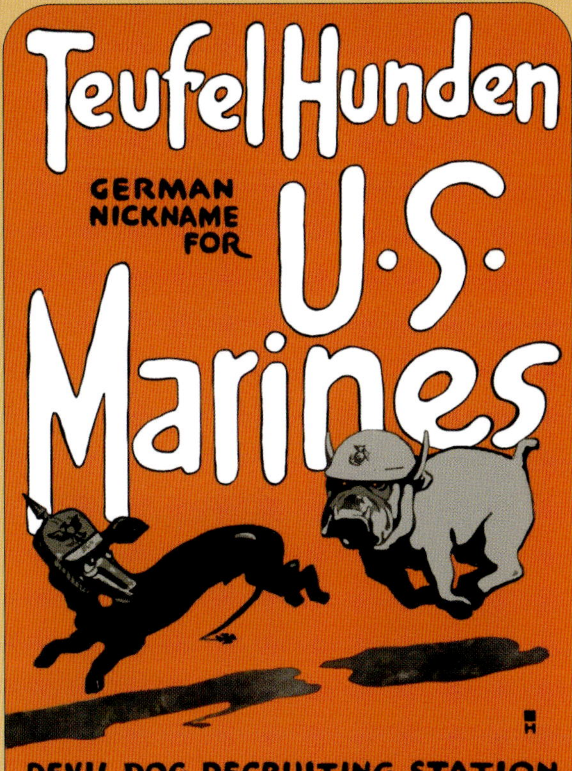

This recruiting poster of a determined American bulldog chasing a German dachshund inspired the U.S. Marines to seek a bulldog to serve as mascot.

(Library of Congress)

Jiggs traveled thousands of miles by plane, ship, car, and train to make promotional appearances.

(U.S. Naval Institute photo archive)

Jiggs II

Dozens of people offered their bulldogs to fill the mascot billet left empty by the death of Jiggs. Heavyweight boxing champion Gene Tunney, a former Marine, offered his own pedigreed bulldog, Silent White Richard, who got the job as Jiggs II. The Marines also accepted a bulldog named Private Padgett gifted by the Royal Marines. Symbolic of the special Anglo-American relationship, the two dogs served as co-mascots. Sadly, Private Padgett seemed unable to acclimate to life in America. He died a year later from heat exhaustion after attending several Marine baseball games. Jiggs II continued as the Marine mascot until 1937.

Jiggs II is suited up and ready to get into the game, circa 1928.

(Marine Corps Archives and Special Collections)

Still wearing his Royal Marine uniform, Private Padgett is transferred into the U.S. Marines in 1927.

(Author's collection)

Chesty

By the time Jiggs VII died in 1960, a new dynasty had begun in Washington, DC, where a bulldog named Chesty was the mascot of the Marine Barracks. Named in honor of highly decorated Lt. Gen. Lewis "Chesty" Puller, Chesty took over the mantle of top Marine bulldog. Though the first Chesty lacked the discipline required of a Marine and had to be sent back to boot camp for additional training, he established a line that has remained unbroken for more than six decades. Chesty XVI reported for mascot duty in 2022.

A new dynasty began when Chesty became the Marine Corps mascot in 1960. This is Chesty III at the Marine Barracks in Washington, DC, which the current line of mascots has called home for more than six decades.

(U.S. Naval Institute photo archive)

Admiral Wags

As he had on several of his other ships, Capt. Frederick Sherman brought along Admiral Wags when he took command of aircraft carrier USS *Lexington.* Throughout the Battle of the Coral Sea in 1942, the black cocker spaniel stayed under the captain's bed and out of the way of the sailors trying to defend the "Lady Lex." After *Lexington* was crippled by several torpedoes and bombs, the men were ordered to abandon ship. Captain Sherman made his way through the smoke-filled passageway to grab Admiral Wags, whom he wrapped in a life jacket and lowered by rope to a rescue vessel. The two were later reunited, and on his return to the United States, Captain Sherman was awarded a special (non–Navy regulation) dog-saving medal by the Tail-Waggers Club of Washington. After the war, Captain Sherman's wife, Fanny, wrote a well-received book about Admiral Wags' adventures in the Navy. Admiral Wags even added his "pawtograph" to a number of copies.

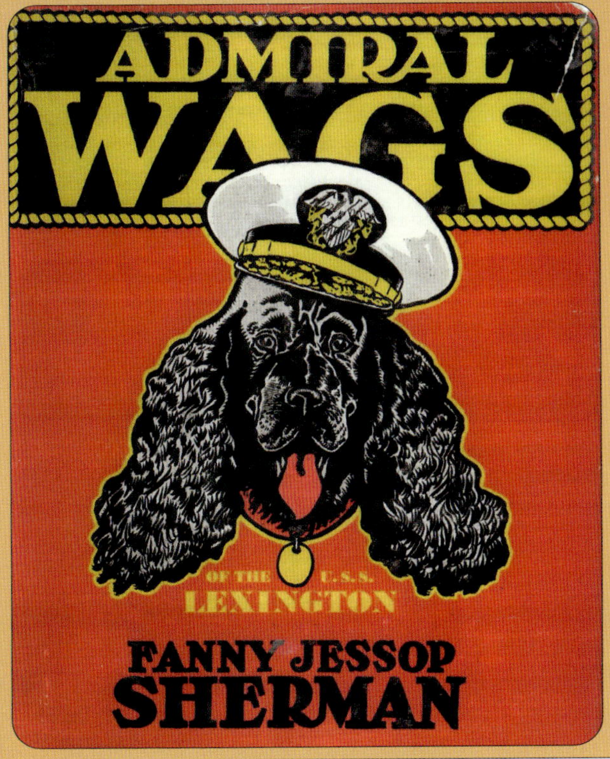

Cover of the book *Admiral Wags* by Fanny Jessop Sherman, wife of Capt. Frederick Sherman.

(Collection of Adm. Harry Harris)

To Margaret Hewlett,
Cordial Greetings!
Fanny Jessop Sherman.
1945.

A Salute!
Admiral Wags.

Admiral Wags autographed copies with his paw print.

(Collection of Adm. Harry Harris)

Bamse

Living up to his name, which meant "teddy bear," Bamse was a huge, affectionate St. Bernard who served on the Norwegian minesweeper *Thorodd* and eventually became the mascot of the entire Norwegian navy during World War II. When Norway surrendered to the Nazis in 1940, *Thorodd* escaped to Scotland, where Bamse ingratiated himself with the locals. He was even given a bus pass, which he wore on his collar. He was frequently seen traveling into town to fetch shipmates who overstayed at the pubs. As Bamse's fame grew, he was elevated to mascot for all of the Free Norwegian Forces. Bamse still watches over Montrose Harbor in Scotland in the form of a life-size bronze statue that was unveiled in 2006.

The huge but sociable Bamse made such an impression on the people of Montrose, Scotland, that they immortalized him with a statue.

(Royal Norwegian Navy)

Melissa

While not quite as famous as the Navy's Bill the goat, Melissa, a schnauzer belonging to the U.S. Naval Academy's football coach, was a popular sight as she ran up and down the sidelines during games in the 1940s. She earned a special place in the hearts of Navy midshipmen when she chased Army's mule at the 1942 Army-Navy game. Melissa wore a blanket emblazoned with five stars denoting each of Navy's wins over Army that she apparently inspired. When Melissa died in 1949, she was buried at the fifty-yard line of Navy's football stadium.

Melissa sits in front of the U.S. Naval Academy's junior varsity football team in 1941. When she passed away in 1949, several former team members who had become senior officers returned to Annapolis for her funeral.

(U.S. Naval Academy)

U.S. Navy ships once carried goats because they could supply the crew with fresh dairy products while requiring less space than cows. These sailors and a Marine pose with their ship's mascot dog and goat, circa 1918.

(Author's collection)

Dodo

Two decades after Melissa died, Dodo ruled Annapolis. A stray of uncertain origin who had meandered onto the Naval Academy Yard, he was truly the dog of all the midshipmen as he slept in a different room every night. Even though officials forbade Dodo from traveling on academy transportation, the midshipmen somehow managed to get him to every football game, both home and away. The story of Dodo and how he was adopted by the entire brigade of midshipmen at the Naval Academy was pitched to Disney for a potential movie, but the studio politely declined due to their full production schedule.

Dodo in his "Bite Army" blanket was a common sight on the sidelines of U.S. Naval Academy sporting events in the late 1960s and early 1970s.

(U.S. Naval Academy)

Liberty Hound

The droopy-eyed basset hound mascot of the minesweeper USS *Pluck* was initially named Commissioner after the fretful character on the 1960s TV show *Batman*. Noticing that the basset became excited at the prospect of going ashore after he smelled land, the crew renamed him Liberty Hound. "Lib" was always in search of affection and conducted regular "inspections," approaching every man on the ship and insisting on being petted. In foreign ports, Lib was a novelty and received plenty of attention from crowds of people who had never seen a basset hound. He developed an appreciation of extra cold beer, so the crew thought it necessary to give him a tag with instructions on how to return him to the ship if he was ever found stumbling about town.

Liberty Hound trying to steer his ship to the nearest port.

(U.S. Naval Institute photo archive)

Sam

In 1953 ammunition ship USS *Wrangell* sighted a ghost ship floundering in the Mediterranean. A boarding party confirmed that the fishing vessel was empty except for an emaciated dog found near the remains of a man who had been dead for two weeks. The fate of the rest of the crew could not be determined. *Wrangell* took the derelict vessel under tow, leaving the gaunt dog on board with food and water because quarantine laws did not allow the American sailors to bring him on board. The ghost vessel was no longer seaworthy, though, and quickly sank. As it slipped beneath the waves, *Wrangell*'s crew spotted the dog struggling in the heavy seas. The captain broke regulations to haul the dog on board. After nursing the animal back to health and making sure that he received all his immunizations, the sailors named him Sam and kept him. Sam became the happy mascot of the ship and the subject of several news stories about the ghost ship and its sad fate.

These eight naval air crewmen and their mascot, Turbo, are in good spirits after escaping a watery death. Their plane went down in the Pacific, but they were quickly rescued by the U.S. Coast Guard.

(NARA)

Judy

An English pointer serving in the Royal Navy on river gunboat HMS *Grasshopper* in Southeast Asia became one of the most remarkable mascots of World War II. Judy survived an attempted dognapping by American sailors, the sinking of two ships, a crocodile attack, a shooting, and capture. After being taken by the Japanese, she earned the distinction of being the only dog registered as a prisoner of war. She also saved the lives of numerous sailors by finding fresh water for shipwreck victims on a deserted island and food for POWs in the Japanese camps. On several occasions, she alerted her human companions to the presence of deadly threats, including a leopard, a tiger, snakes, and scorpions. Upon being liberated from a camp in 1945, Judy was sent to the United Kingdom, where she was welcomed as a hero. For her gallantry, Judy was awarded the Dicken Medal, the highest honor given animals serving the British empire.

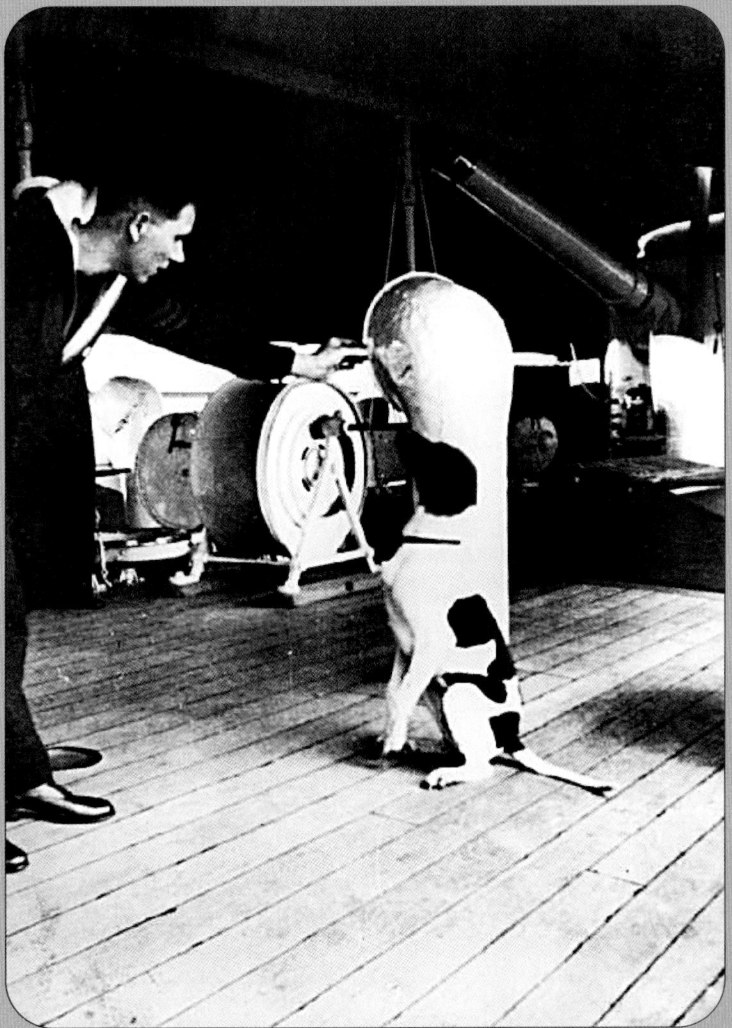

The bravery and loyalty of Judy would be tested throughout World War II. The English pointer's survival instincts saved the lives of her human companions on several occasions.

(Imperial War Museum)

Just Nuisance

The only dog ever to be officially enlisted in the Royal Navy was an enormous Great Dane named Just Nuisance, the mascot of the base in Simonstown, South Africa. The dog was named Nuisance because he was always underfoot blocking entrances with his large frame. Nuisance never went to sea, but sailors managed to finagle enlistment papers for him so that he could travel with them on the train when they went to the pub. Just Nuisance is fondly remembered by the residents of Simonstown, where a statue of him now stands.

Though playful and friendly with sailors, Just Nuisance was destined for shore duty because of his towering size.

(Australian War Memorial)

Error of the Terror

Error was only a tiny pup when he was smuggled onto the minelayer USS *Terror* in a sailor's peacoat pocket in 1942. The puppy grew into a large and loyal "chief dog" of the ship. When Error was in a foreign port and got involved in fierce fights for the affections of a female dog, sailors took pride in the fact that Error almost always won the girl. He gained further respect when he survived a kamikaze strike during the Battle of Okinawa. When *Terror* was deactivated after the war, Error was transferred to the destroyer tender USS *Arcadia*. As it happened, *Arcadia* ended up tied next to *Terror*. Error recognized his former ship and continued to protect it by barking at anyone who dared to step foot on it.

Tuffy was the mascot of the minesweeper USS *Competent* when he wasn't on MP duty. Like Error of the Terror, Tuffy was a loyal dog, but sometimes got into trouble. He spotted a female dog on another nearby ship as *Competent* was getting underway and promptly went over the side into the water. He was recovered and later got an assignment on dry land as mascot of the Marine Detachment at NavBase Charleston, South Carolina.

(U.S. Navy)

Soochow

Soochow was a stray mutt found in Shanghai and was adopted by the Fourth Marine Regiment as a mascot in 1937. Soochow accompanied the Marines when they were sent to the Philippines in 1941. The dog survived the Battle of Corregidor and joined the other prisoners of war on the Bataan Death March. Though the captured Marines were starving in the prison camps, they shared their meager rations with their loyal dog. By the time the camps were liberated in 1945, Soochow's weight had dropped from thirty pounds to eleven. As the Marines were preparing to sail back to the United States, they learned that the ships were at capacity and Soochow would not be allowed to board. Desperate for home after spending more than three years in a prison camp, one of the Marines nevertheless refused to leave without Soochow. An officer intervened and arranged for the Marine and Soochow to fly to California, where Soochow recovered and resumed his duties as the Fourth Marines' mascot in San Diego.

Because Soochow had proven himself so loyal to his companions held as POWs in the Philippines, his Marine buddy refused to return to the United States without him when they were liberated.

(Marine Corps Archives and Special Collections)

Caesar

Caesar was donated to the military by a family who recognized his special qualities. The Marines trained the German shepherd to be a messenger, and he was an integral member of the team. His handlers even placed his pawprints on their letters home. During the Bougainville campaign in 1943, Caesar made nine messenger trips in two days, keeping communications open between a Marine company and the battalion command post thirty-one miles away. When Caesar attacked a Japanese soldier who was attempting to throw a grenade, he was shot in the chest and leg. His handler rushed Caesar to a surgeon, who tended to the wounded dog but was unable to remove a bullet that was lodged near Caesar's heart. Caesar made a full recovery after three weeks and reported back for duty, still carrying the bullet next to his heart.

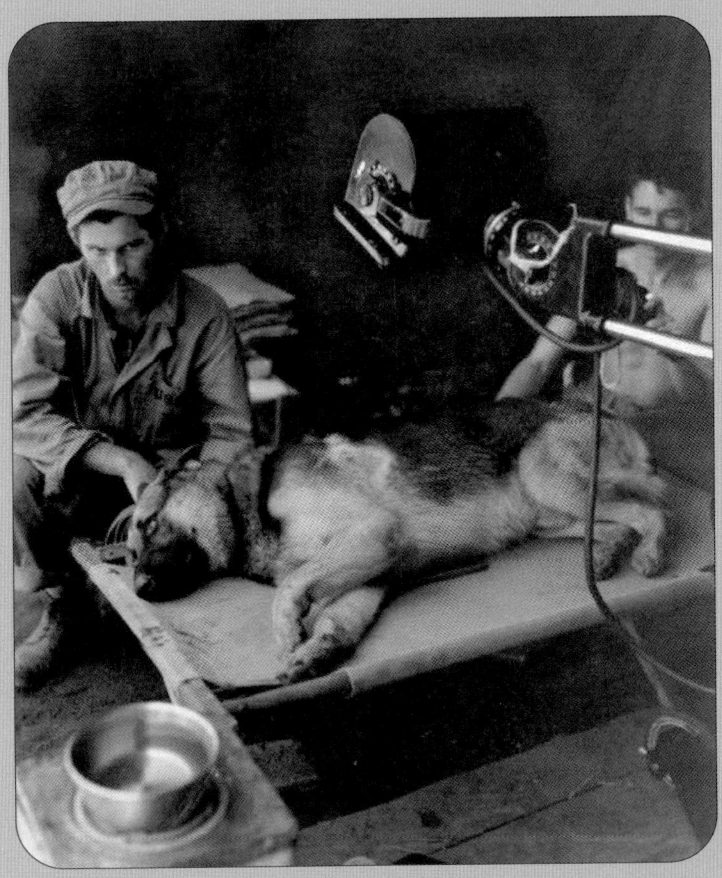

His worried handler watches as a Navy corpsman X-rays Caesar. The German shepherd was shot twice but recovered from his wounds.

(NARA)

Cairo

Cairo, a Belgian Malinois, took part in one of the most famous missions in recent special forces history. A working dog assigned to U.S. Navy SEALs fighting the war on terror, Cairo was noted for his uncanny ability to differentiate friend from foe. In 2011 Cairo was chosen to participate in Operation Neptune Spear, the raid to eliminate Osama bin Laden. When the SEAL teams' helicopters landed at bin Laden's compound in Pakistan, with one helicopter crashing during the descent, Cairo was unleashed to search for traps and escape tunnels while the SEALs cleared the house and killed the notorious terrorist. Cairo then guarded the damaged helicopter until the SEALs could remove all the sensitive equipment on board. When Cairo was retired in 2013, he was adopted by his handler, Will Chesney.

Cairo with his handler, Navy SEAL Will Chesney. When Cairo was retired by the Navy, Chesney adopted the dog to help him cope with his own PTSD.

(U.S. Navy)

Jim Texas

During World War I, Royal Navy admiral David Beatty signaled to U.S. Navy ships on station with the British Grand Fleet that he had a Staffordshire bull terrier puppy available for any crew in need of a mascot. All the U.S. Navy ships signaled back that they wanted the pup, but battleship USS *Texas* took no chances and immediately sent a boat to HMS *Queen Elizabeth* to claim the dog. The British-born terrier was given the all-American name of Jim Texas. Jim considered himself a senior officer and preferred to lounge in the battleship's wardroom. He liked to engage the officers by carrying a penny in his mouth and then dropping it at their feet. The officer chosen to play the game would kick the penny, and Jim Texas would scramble after it. Jim enjoyed the game so much that he slept with a penny in his mouth.

Mascots rarely concerned themselves with the rank of their shipmates as long as they received ample attention, but Jim Texas preferred the company of officers.

(U.S. Navy)

Zero

A small white fox terrier who joined battleship USS *Washington* when he was only a month old earned the devotion of the crew during World War II. In addition to being amused by Zero's playful antics, like chasing ocean spray on deck, the sailors respected Zero's fearlessness when he encountered dogs from other ships, watching with pride when he barked at larger rival mascots. Like most sea dogs, Zero had occasional lapses in discipline. He once faced a captain's mast for "being unsanitary in an unauthorized part of the ship." As punishment, Zero received five days' confinement on bread and water with a bone on the third day. Zero disappeared when the ship was docked in New York City after the war.

At the end of the war, Zero disappeared while his ship, USS *Washington*, was docked in New York. Whether he walked away to start life as a civilian dog or a separating sailor decided to take him home, no one knows.

(Author's collection)

Spar

Spar was a Boston terrier with a career worthy of an action hero. Adopted as a pup by the Coast Guard, Spar went to war on the cutter *Spencer*. She was on the *Spencer* when in 1943 the ship sank *U-175* as the German submarine was attempting to attack a convoy in the North Atlantic. Apparently, however, action at sea was not enough for Spar, because she became one of the few dogs of the era to earn jump wings after she had to bail out of a crippled plane and parachuted to safety in the arms of a Coast Guardsman.

Spar of the U.S. Coast Guard cutter *Spencer*. Spar's airborne leap was an unusual accomplishment for a dog during World War II, but today's Navy SEALS and Marines train dogs to skydive with a handler or fast-rope from helicopters.

(U.S. Navy)

Notes

1. Virginia Morrel, "From Wolf to Dog," *Scientific American* 313, 1 (July 2015), 60-67.

2. *Cedar Rapids Gazette*, November 25, 1943, p. 28.

3. *Biloxi Daily Herald*, October 14, 1944, p. 2.

4. Joshua Levine, "The Education of a Bomb Dog," *Smithsonian Magazine*, July 2013.

About the Author

SCOT CHRISTENSON is the director of communications for the U.S. Naval Institute. He began his career as a television producer and journalist before going on to develop and manage media strategies for a wide range of organizations, including amusement parks, zoos, think tanks, and lobbying firms. He has written about history and pop culture for several periodicals and frequently serves as a consultant on television and film productions. He lives in Alexandria, Virginia, with his wife.

The Naval Institute Press is the book-publishing arm of the U.S. Naval Institute, a private, nonprofit, membership society for sea service professionals and others who share an interest in naval and maritime affairs. Established in 1873 at the U.S. Naval Academy in Annapolis, Maryland, where its offices remain today, the Naval Institute has members worldwide.

Members of the Naval Institute support the education programs of the society and receive the influential monthly magazine *Proceedings* or the colorful bimonthly magazine *Naval History* and discounts on fine nautical prints and on ship and aircraft photos. They also have access to the transcripts of the Institute's Oral History Program and get discounted admission to any of the Institute-sponsored seminars offered around the country.

The Naval Institute's book-publishing program, begun in 1898 with basic guides to naval practices, has broadened its scope to include books of more general interest. Now the Naval Institute Press publishes about seventy titles each year, ranging from how-to books on boating and navigation to battle histories, biographies, ship and aircraft guides, and novels. Institute members receive significant discounts on the Press' more than eight hundred books in print.

Full-time students are eligible for special half-price membership rates. Life memberships are also available.

For a free catalog describing Naval Institute Press books currently available, and for further information about joining the U.S. Naval Institute, please write to:

Member Services
U.S. Naval Institute
291 Wood Road
Annapolis, MD 21402-5034
Telephone: (800) 233-8764
Fax: (410) 571-1703
Web address: www.usni.org